1990

TORQUE

1987

Agnes Lynch Starrett

Poetry Prize

DAVID RIVARD

Torque

University of Pittsburgh Press

Published by the University of Pittsburgh Press, Pittsburgh, Pa. 15260
Copyright © 1988, David Rivard
All rights reserved
Feffer and Simons, Inc., London
Manufactured in the United States of America

Library of Congress Cataloging in Publication Data

Rivard, David, 1953–
Torque.

(Pitt poetry series)
I. Title. II. Series.
PS3568.I8285T67   1988   811'.54   88-2167
ISBN 0-8229-3595-3
ISBN 0-8229-5410-9 (pbk.)

Earlier versions of these poems appeared in: *The Agni Review* ("Ariadne," "Arrival Song," "Firestone," and "The Road Out"); *The Black Warrior Review* ("Walking By"); *Crazyhorse* ("The Fast Long Time," "Lies," and "The Venice of the North"); *5 AM* ("Masks" and "To the God"); *Indiana Review* ("How It Will Always Seem" and "The Temptations"); *Ironwood* ("1966" and "Simon Says"); *The North American Review* ("Fall River"); *Poetry East* ("Leaving the Gateway Cinema"); *Shankpainter* ("Consolation," "The Mission," "One Reason," "One Too Many Mornings," and "Torque"); *Sonora Review* ("Cures," "Secured Town," and "There"); *Telescope* ("Double Indemnity"); and *Tendril* ("Late?").

Besides those whose names appear on these pages, I'd like to thank Jon Anderson, Peter Behrens, Tess Gallagher, Anne Makepeace, Steve Orlen, Michael Ryan, and Michaela Sullivan for their help with these poems, for their encouragement and friendship.

To Tony Hoagland, absolute gratitude *and the light for friends.*

I am especially grateful to the Fine Arts Work Center in Provincetown, and to the National Endowment for the Arts, for grants which helped me finish this book.

*The publication of this book is supported by grants
from the National Endowment for the Arts
in Washington, D.C., a Federal agency,
and the Pennsylvania Council on the Arts.*

Michaela

"The sense of justice is an enemy of prayer. How to ask for a miracle if innumerable human beings, just like yourself, begged and it was refused to them? Very well, but is it really worthwhile to force oneself to be so just? To pretend to be superhuman? An angel?"

—Czeslaw Milosz

Contents

I

Contents

II

How It Will Always Seem

—for David Guenette

Last night in Fall River in Lafayette Park,
Near a dilapidated tin tot-slide, and after
He'd snorted angel dust, my friend wanted to swing
At me with a two-by-four. Both of us sweating

Like crazy. For one brief moment, on that glass-
Wracked playground asphalt, a transitory
Instant, it seemed something—pure, engaging—
Which he despised on sight and wanted to smash,

Had revealed itself. But, look, it was really
Just two girls in cut-offs and halter tops.
They'd drunk and flirted with us all night.
Not visions, holy or demonic, even with other-worldly

And soulful tans. They had those bleached
Shag-cuts easy to make fun of, easy for me anyway.
Who knows what I said. But they took off,
And he got pissed. I don't care what he saw.

I down my cornflakes this morning, stare
At puffy red roses on the kitchen wallpaper.
Can't find my gloves, and meanwhile I'm late
For punch-in at the dye plant. So, outside,

I pretend at first I don't hear my father call
From his pickup. Road grit, bugs on the windshield.
On the dash, a crumpled race form: what's left
Of win-or-else shouts as three-year-olds hit

The wire at Suffolk Downs: a scream to be lifted clear,
Now. *Nothing*, I tell him, leaning on the truck door,
When he asks what I did last night. When what
He means is *what are you trying to prove, pal?*

And *smarten-up*. This is how it will always seem to me.
As if a father always knows when his son lies,
And the son lies because he's sure of nothing
But the fact he's headed toward a factory,

Not even noticing why work is noisy and lonely
As the inside of a skull, or what drifts down
Into your blood from convoluted piping
Around fabric vats, or why that river flows

Past the plant, until, reaching sea twenty miles
Down, near a sand bar, it loses itself,
Now, while the beach haze starts to burn off.
While the day, swallow-delighting, already

Humid, shimmers like a smudged, heavy coin.

1966

Innocence? Soon as you try putting your finger on it
it zips off, a blur, like a slot car
plastered with oil and tire company decals,
like the low-slung Formula One winners that two boys,
thirteen, race over banked curves
and flats colored the tarmac gray of thunder clouds—
a track the olive-skinned boy built to mimic
the Daytona Grand Prix. Cool basement air,
ozone rasp of electric motors;
they hunch juicing the cars with black joysticks.

Across the room under old magazines is a book.
But the dark kid—he's pudgy, his mother says "baby fat"—
well, he can't decide to tell his friend
about it. And beneath this debate with himself
swim images of sullen fashion models
from the book's trashy, softcore, uptown romances.
Words, vaguely glamorous, like *valium*,
coitus interruptus, pouting girls, naked, half-naked,
all riding surging currents of possessiveness
or shame or ache until they fuse, inevitably,
into need. The need he feels, however
confusing, for secret. So that he bursts out, laughing,
punching, happily blaming the other boy
when, at a crisscross, their sleek racers smash up.

Later, his friend, a sandy-haired wiseass,
stands near the workbench littered by airplane kits,
plastic carcasses. He fiddles with a crimped tube of epoxy.
Hung on string, a camouflage-
coated B-52 banks above his head. Above a valley
and burning trucks and bodies, fires blending with sunlight
while the sun passes on to the next wilderness or pasture.

5

And, if only to buy that last line,
two boys smear the inside of a Stop & Shop bag with glue.
All right, says one, stick your head in.
Doesn't the darker boy tip his face to the sack?
Soon his chubby little heart seems to slam
not just in his chest but within the dim bag,
as, each long breath, the bag collapses and swells,
as if his heart pleads to punch out an opening, a hole.
Soon it does, soon
the fragrant and careless light streams in.

Fall River

When I wake now it's below ocherous, saw-ridged
pine beams. Haze streaks all three windows. I look up
at the dog-eared, glossy magazine photo
I've taken with me for years. It gets tacked
like a claim to some new wall in the next place—
Bill Russell & Wilt Chamberlain, one on one
the final game of the 1969 NBA championship,
two hard men snapped elbowing & snatching at a basketball
as if it were a moment one of them might stay inside
forever. I was with
my father the night that game played
on a fuzzy color television, in a jammed Fall River bar.
Seagram & beer chasers for hoarse ex-jocks,
smoke rifting the air. A drunk called him "Tiger"
and asked about the year he'd made all-state guard—
point man, ball-hawk, pacer. Something he rarely spoke
of, & almost always with a gruff mix of impatience
and shyness. Each year,
days painting suburban tract houses & fighting
with contractors followed by
night shifts at the fire station
followed by his kids swarming at breakfast
and my mother trying to stay out of his way,
each of the many stone-hard moments between 1941 & 1969—
they made up a city of granite mills
by a slate & blue river. That town was my father's
life, & still is. If he felt cheated by it,
by its fate for him,
to bear that disappointment, he kept it secret.
                                              That
night, when he stared deep into a drunk's memory,
he frowned. He said nothing. He twisted on the stool,
and ordered this guy a beer.

Whatever my father & I have in common
is mostly silence. And anger that keeps twisting
back on itself, though not before it ruins,
often, even something simple
as a walk in the dunes at a warm beach.
But what we share too is a love so awkward
that it explains, with unreasoning perfection,
why we still can't speak
easily to each other, about the past or anything else,
and why I wake this far from the place where I grew up,
while the wall above me claims now
nothing has changed & all is different.

Torque

After his ham & cheese in the drape factory cafeteria,
having slipped by the bald shipping foreman
to ride a rattling elevator to the attic
where doves flicker into the massive eaves
and where piled boxes of out-of-style
cotton and lace won't ever be
decorating anyone's sun parlor windows.
Having dozed off in that hideout he fixed
between five four-by-six cardboard storage cartons
while the rest of us pack Mediterranean Dreams
and Colonial Ruffles and drapes colored like moons,
and he wakes lost—
shot through
into a world of unlocked unlocking light—
suddenly he knows where he is and feels half nuts
and feels like killing some pigeons with a slingshot.

That's all, and that's why he pokes
his calloused fingers into the broken machinery,
hunting for loose nuts a half inch wide—
five greasy cold ones that warm in his pocket—
and yanks back the snag-cut strip of inner tube
with a nut snug at the curve to snap it
at the soft chest of a dopey bird.
Then the noise of pigeons flopping down
to creosoted hardwood, and then a grin
the guy gives me & all his other pals later.
And afternoon tightens down on all
our shoulders, until the shift whistle
blasts, blowing through the plant like air
through lace. As it always has, as it does.
That bright. That stunned.

Firestone

Who would want to die defending Firestone Tire
and its brick storage yards?
That night, at a plant torched by two laid-off steamfitters,
crawling the maze of a shipping dock, dazed, choking
on the floor with an empty oxygen tank,
my father would be discovered by another firefighter,
who would half-lead, half-drag him
by his collar to the outside.
No, my father didn't want to die there,
not even if every seed, each grain of sand, *is* numbered.
Just as ten years later nothing could explain it to him —
just why the man who'd saved him lay comatose
in a semi-private hospital room,
cancer resculpting every cell in his liver.
For weeks my father went around
wearing a miserable, distracted look,
as though carrying on constant arguments with fate,
as if it were some sentient lump or a postulating, querulous
wind loud as the Machine Age
furnace squatting at home in the basement corner.
At night, when its oil burners kicked on,
a glow filtered out the access hatch,
heavy glass the size of a dollar bill,
deep orange, flickering slightly, suffused.
Floorboards and air would hum. A base rumble that,
to my father, may have seemed filled with every loss
put in this world, to deny us, to crush.
The hell with that. He smashed a beer bottle
against the cellar wall. No cry for help.
The hell with that. Nine years old, the only thing I'd heard
when my father, back from Firestone, pushed into our house,

was the groan of the couch. Smoke and creosote,
stink of burning rubber. Soot
blackened his hair, soot eyebrows, soot forehead.
I'd stayed awake, listening as he nodded off and snored,
somehow imagining ash
got sucked into his lungs, or deeper.
How deep could it go?

One Too Many Mornings

After working the midtown ambulance night slot,
my brother drinks in a tavern, his back to thin bars
of lacquered sunlight, venetian blinds. In jeans
and a flannel cowboy shirt, & trying to down-shift
enough to head home. He sips a bourbon.
It carries him a little ways off,
not far enough. How can I get out, he thinks.
On the raised television, an ugly, yellow, manic cartoon bird
keeps escaping its cage,
only to be recaptured. No sound. But his partner, Franco,
jokes about this brunette emergency room nurse.
How she doesn't wear panties, how she asks
Does that mean you like me? when he stares too long.
My brother has heard it all before,
so the reply is an echo. One bad joke
then another. It's like asking *why*
when you know the one right answer is to repeat
the question. Why, last night, at the Hyatt

glitter palace, he had to pull a limp twelve-year-old
from the heated, chlorine-stinking swimming pool.
He fingered the carotid for a pulse. It was there,
it wasn't. Some blood flecked an earlobe.
Kitchen noise, banged pots. Shouts from a distance.
Then a small crowd, uneasy murmurs.
When he locked fists & struck the boy's chest,
trying to make the heart flutter, switch on,
the rib cage cracked. A grunt came from the mouth,
a laugh, then silence. A laugh, he said. That's
what he remembers. Nobody
shut off the pool lights. The warm blue-green
planets under water became more
and more still, simplified & quiet.

Like a man in a bar who just doesn't want to talk,
because there are many wrong answers,
ways to soften failure. And no one wrong or close
enough, no one as far away as he is.

The Venice of the North

For a while then I lived near the old
town, Gamla Stan, and each day I walked down
along the barge canals for a few hours.
Early winter, cobblestone turning into snow.
There was a day it flurried and I watched

students near a government building protest,
chanting their demands, a small bunch.
There was a tourist hotel in a square
where three prostitutes huddled drinking tea,
cold, breath rising, two of them arm in arm,

as anonymous as anyone could desire.
The tall one who looked about my age
glanced at me for a moment, why should
I be alone today? The whole city, each corner,
seemed to ask something, and each feeling

had become a question I asked myself.
And if there are cities I won't see again,
who can prove my answers back then were lies?
Not lies, really, but things I should have said
and never did. No lies, yet. Blown by wind

the snow would rise in odd twists through
lighted rows of high apartment windows.
I knew a woman living in a place nearby.
If I wanted to, I could imagine her
switching off the radio, getting up

from the couch to sort her clothes into piles
of laundry. A red wool shirt. She'd peer at it,
a brass button on the sleeve—what shape was
pressed in it, an anchor, crossed swords?—
then she'd toss it and slam the door.

Her name was Vera and she was slowly
going blind. She did some sort of work
at a little seafood restaurant
near the start of the suburbs: behind it
the bay froze in winter and you could walk

on the ice. Once, killing time until
her shift ended, I went out as far
as a channel marker. When I looked back toward
a hill outlined by bare maple, I remembered
the newspaper, pictures of a new work camp,

how carefully a barbed wire fence had been
hidden behind a grove of trees. We were reading
about it at breakfast—I was reading parts
out loud to her—when she laughed
and said going blind was like a trial

for political crimes. Drawn out so the
citizenry can learn from your example.
A guard brings out two needles, light pink
with fluid, pricks you, and you think you're dead.
Later on, you wake, the cell is dark,

a voice is asking, *Now will you behave yourself?*
I never told her I loved her. I thought
it was a lie. Of course, there is a lie
inside my memory of this. And I
did love her. But was afraid. It got so

twisted up. The last time I saw her, on
my way, I passed a porno shop
window, where an advertisement hung,
the Swedish word for *punishment* flaring
into a photo of two people lying

15

across each other in bed. In the glass,
among contraptions of love, I stared back.
Then a store peddling shoes, a wall of them
rose into the sky, wooden and leather clogs,
a way of walking, vanishing, snowlike,

above the islanded city of Stockholm,
the Venice of the North. The third Venice being
memory, the punishment for certain questions.

Consolation

—for Dianne

There is none. And this means today,
Saturday, I have a reason to walk 24th Street.
Chromed lowrides jam by for *chicas*.
And if you needed reasons this badly
you'd linger too, watching an early sixties
white Chevy convertible, streaming cool brilliance,
as it trails a nineteen-year-old sales clerk who swished out
the Tico House of Beauty. Silver crucifix earrings,
razor-cut hair, magenta lipstick. And over Prince funking
from the radio's blast, when they call to her, *Valerie,*
I swear, it almost might sound to you like, *Hey,*
pal of the dream! But I've lived eight months
in this district, lots of jittery eyes, laughing,
kids wailing at bus stops. No rapture. Scraps
of newsprint, kleenex, candy wrappers snap
across the intersection. Strange that a wind this strong
makes shoppers seem strong trudging into it.
Someone stops to ask me a question in Spanish,
near the library, & I can't answer. Near somebody
bundled in fake mink, wool scarf,
shivering in eighty-degree heat, brown hand scribbling
furiously across greasy, ruled notepaper,
erasing the minutes. Never mind what fury it is
that drives the pen, I can't tell if it's a woman or man.
Why shouldn't I admit I don't understand? Not the question,
not the cold body bent over, or anyone else's
indecipherable life.
                    Each day, brackish & shining,
the bay swings twice to the ocean, twice back.
Every night at dusk the hillsides of condos & homes flicker on
above Castro. Enough for me to think, sure, those lights
will go on every day. Until my next thought

17

shuts them off, a scratch on crumpled paper
that reports some days everything stops. The day
my friend lost her baby,
her small body tearing itself up. And that pain
can't be undone, or held down. I'd been writing her a letter.
I couldn't think what to say. Went out,
the morning hot, windy. There's a slick guy
stuck at a traffic light, gunning his engine.
I have to listen—like a heartbeat after an accident,
racing, racing.

The Road Out

There's an infinity of choices,

But Carlos & Schweidel & I don't know it when we hit on heading
For this bar off Speedway. The road here four lanes

Of sodium vapor lamps & palmettos & shifting accelerations,
Then a parking lot beneath The Blue Note's blinking red neon.
We walk into canned rock 'n' roll where, twenty-five hours a day,

Just as the sign says, three gorgeous coeds
Strip & purr in sexual abandon, or dance bored silly & degraded,
Depending on who you ask. If you bother,

Which we don't. So, as we take out our money,

The bilious little clear-eyed patriot on each dollar
Agrees it is better sometimes to rest
Inside sweet incomprehension, not knowing who you are

When you are a man in the crowd who barks barking his laugh,
When you are an illusion who asks each table to tip her dance.

Better that a biker with tangled beard & leather top hat
Get up when the blue spot invades his heart & lick
A tattered five-dollar bill
So as to paste it more easily

On the sumptuous belly of the woman twitching low now on stage.
It is better, because no one here prays to become someone else,
And if they did, it would only be to beg
Let me, Let me become, Let me become the name of the road out.

Ariadne

You, of the voice always teasing & throaty in asking
if I'd do anything you wanted—and who wouldn't—
you & I heard. Word was
it didn't cost much. Just climb the cracked linoleum stairs
and look for the nine-ball tables,
Bobby's territory. Bobby, His Highness, Mister Baby.
The huaraches, the graying muttonchops & chainsmoker's smile
which had somehow coalesced into this small-time dealer,
one who appreciated, deeply, the fools buying his quaaludes,
synthesized pig-tranq that shred
or corroded innumerable nerve-endings,
his kingdom. His fingers, that night, unbuttoning
a pastel Hawaiian shirt so we could stare
at his bypass scars, still bruised purplish & yellow
where the rib-spreader dug in & spread him open,
showing off, making ceremony of it, a ritual,
like the one we would come to later, at your apartment,
when we'd kiss, & you'd pass a quaalude to my tongue.
We would split a shot of mezcal, & next kiss
you'd suck one of the tart, phosphorescent tabs off my lip.
Fits of helpless giggling,
giggling & false starts, mouth distracted by who knows what
on its way to a nipple, knees slipping off the armchair,
until the drug nudged us into that choreography, barely conscious,
that flush kids feel when being
watched over at play. And the one watching?
Probably, I'd have said your husband,
who'd walked out on you, & who was my friend.
All of it some purposeful dance of revenge,
myself in the starring role, the instrument or, better, weapon—
no doubt I actually saw it that way.

Didn't it make irrefutable sense out of the life
I'd walked up to? My life. How much easier to feel that,
and to fall asleep stroking your thigh,
before the sunlight sliced
through your bedroom windows, come its cold blue distance
singing like the hammered iron tip of a spear.

Double Indemnity

All day the rain
washes down and gushes by
my friend Danny Mota's Cadillac
Coupe de Ville, a long
and fat mosquito blue.
There is a movie in which a rain like this,
but conceptualized as fate,
seduction, and murderous lies,
sweeps
over an apartment building
in the Los Angeles basin. A moment
I am convinced Hollywood came upon purely
by luck. A woman with blond hair
stands in a darkened kitchenette and
stops talking—her face lit by neon
flaring through a jalousie window
beams the innocence of a girl.
A girl who has swayed a man
of null will to help murder her husband.
The winding, downhill road
from her stucco and tile townhouse
to his rooms—from nothing-to-worry-about
to everything-gone-wrong—
is honeysuckle lined.
How could he have known honeysuckle
is sometimes the smell of death? How much is instinct
in what Hollywood knows about us
and how much a blind guess at what draws us
to windows where nothing means more than a storm?
They didn't see Mota's
Cadillac up on blocks and Dan solo
in his house high on pills
just so he forgets his job guarding criminals
who are soulless,

who average a bit more than seventeen years
on the planet and who love
like the rest of us to sit in a darkened movie
house breathless with wonder.
Yesterday, after Danny's retriever died
because someone with a board or shovel
bashed in its shameless golden head,
Hollywood didn't offer a reason.
They offered, on television, a late-night movie
which we watched until the end,
until a man slumps, near death,
by a set of glass doors, about to drown
in some rough reality.

The Mission

Look, I'm like everyone else
in this crush. A line of commuters,
rushing, pouring down subway stairs,
like trains shot down the black tube
to Daly City. Each holds a ticket back
from what eight hours of work cost.
In the packed aisle
on the train a man & woman chat:
he wants a brandy, she hopes Ray
has the disco in mind for tonight.
Something is eating at me
and I get lost for awhile
in a parallel dark the window offers.
And during this time that man
daydreaming of cognac gets off,
and so does his daydream
of being no one's career.
Then his Latino typist, a paper bag
swinging in her red-nailed fingers
like a boyfriend's hand.
Then my stop. What if
whatever is eating at me,
whatever black space would like
to swallow me now, made me forget
all that I love
until it became remote & fuzzy?
So that it was like the music I can't
quite hear, the funk that's pouring
into a sweating Walkman boy,
as he rides ahead of me on the escalator
at 24th Street—the Mission—
though the beat is clear & he nods & moves
to it, an assent, his pleasure hard-earned,
a dance.

Hecatombic Blues

"Sounds, like, really loud down there, doesn't it?"
yips my chubby next door neighbor, stoned Debra,
up on the grassy brow of Bernal Heights.
Because the fireworks shooting-off on streets below us,
the hammerheads, bottle rockets & racketing string of salutes,
offer more of a treat than the wan barrage of shells
at the city's far-off, over-orchestrated, official
4th of July.
             But all of us on this crowded, windy hilltop
ought to be allowed to drift away by ourselves,
like smoke which used to be an explosion.
Before it becomes clear what birthright
is ours, what sacrifice we've really been enticed
to & where. I don't say *will be allowed.*
I say *ought to be.*
             Before one of history's blessed
cousins, my nasally cousin, your omniscient brother—
I mean, of course, Deb's husband—turns, grinning, & says,
"Yeah, but if it was war, we'd all have fuckin' Uzi pistols,
man, we'd nail them Libyans!"

Late?

—for George Shelton

Sometimes everything feels like a trick.
Some days things seem to have been stolen from you.
Cash to pay the bills, your sense of humor, friendship.
You could almost believe those are what you look for
as you walk around your neighborhood. But, no, instead, you get
splashes of zinnias against stucco, cactus wrens,
a pack of kids who ignore the sodium amber streetlights
which just stuttered on, because it means their mothers
want them home right this minute. And, on the corner variety
store's wall, a crude, sun-washed mural of the angel Gabriel
defaced by thick black sideburns so he looks like a street punk,
a strutting cholo, so he seems the only creature on earth
who hasn't heard the news that everything can be lost.
His strong upper arms curving naked and graceful
as the tan thighs of a slender, athletic girl.
A girl he's after, though she's gotten bored waiting
on the stoop and watching the sun set behind the foothills.
Sky reddening until it slams into a blue that blesses
anyone oblivious to all the negations,
including the one, pal, where you think it's possible
to step out of your heart and leave it empty as
an egg shell or a cardboard box.

When you finally return home
the tint of sky more or less matches the flash
of a thrush as it swoops from limb to branch,
acacia to willow. Standing at the kitchen counter,
you pick through a carton of strawberries.
Good juicy ones from the moldy and over-ripe.
Choices that are easy. What do you trust anymore?
The aproned man in the mercado said California strawberries,

they're the best this time of year. In bed, later,
you remember the grocer, round belly under his apron,
but as you start, nearly asleep, to tell your wife about him,
how he talked about his deals, she starts
reading aloud from a tattered bird guide, that the wood thrush
is "essentially useful and worthwhile."
What is worthwhile?   Now, remember.

Sometimes

If it is neither a day when our love
earns a lucky ease
nor a day when the smallest word slams in
like a flurry of counterpunches,
but, maybe, one when you look bored,
I go back to that afternoon we first met.
At a backyard party. June light magnified by thin
haze. We talked for hours, the words
by now impossible to catch. But
if we hadn't talked so long, the sun might not
have burned the skin just below your collarbone,
hot red & raw to touch, blistered,
that splash of freckles abandoned
and left naked by your tank top.
So next morning, after breakfast,
I wouldn't have brought you to the emergency room.
The corridor filled
with the worried, annoyed eyes of accidents,
which were stared into & promised something
by an intern whose wire frames kept
slipping down his nose. After, because wind
cooled the burn, you wanted
to drive around
with the convertible top down.
First a promise, then roads lined by elm
stretching over themselves to touch.

Vapor Lock

She leaves through the smoked-glass doors, the automatic
    kind that hiss open, hiss shut.
Lanky, a woozy gracefulness in her printed skirt, crossing
    the waves of shimmering heat off the parking lot tarmac.
Later, perhaps, she'll blame the sedatives, or blind haste, maybe
    even grief for foolishness—but, whatever,
    on a hot day she shouldn't pump the gas pedal.
All week Los Angeles has hovered near one hundred degrees.
The Toyota catches, then seizes and stalls.
Gas line choked, so she has to sit and wait while the line
    clears.
Only a matter, say, of fifteen minutes.
Say fifteen lifetimes, when all she wants is to get away
    from this clinic where she has just had an abortion.
As quickly as possible. You can understand that, can't you?
The shade of a chopped, ornamental palm slices over the car,
    and she opens the door, slight breeze then.
And, just as if someone had absent-mindedly turned an ignition
    switch somewhere, only what starts is a thought
    she has about the baby.
Would it have had her mouth or her husband's?
The ornamental palm goes on slicing, oblivious, through the car,
    across the tears on her face now, and then over
    her childhood as she starts to sleep lightly in the seat
    and is swept back into a dream she had again and again
    for several months when she was about ten:
    in an intensely bright operating room arena, her father
    out on the table, while she's left alone with him.
You, from where you are, even you might feel the aura's arc,
    from the ivory wall tile of the clinic
    to the dream's fluorescent hospital.

But you are not her father, who came to wake and calm her
  those times, soothing.
And the wind?
When the breeze gusts and swirls now it isn't concerned
  with the fitfully dozing woman in this
  beat-up blue car.
It's blown from far away, gone someplace farther.

Lies

I'm not surprised
to find myself humming a tune I heard once
when I was nineteen. Some swing beat
at a wedding party. I was best man,
tag end of a humid Saturday in September.
Once in a while the groom's eyes got this wild look,
as if one of many older men shaking hands
with him had tried to crush his fingers
while he stood there
in a foppish gray cutaway coat,
his wispy red hair tied in a ponytail.
But the bride, sweet, dark,
from money, kept circling back to kiss him.
And when I started my toast
the guests halted the swirl
of celebration, already more like a photo of guests
around serving plates full of roast and melon,
fresh-cut mums and flown-in orchids. In that pause
the lifted wine glasses glinted like anxious flames,
flames that are easy to see through.
And later my friend and his wife danced,
a little drunk, on the porch.
The horn section lurching through
the song. They danced.

I could tell you now their clumsiness
seemed briefly to imply a terrifying premonition
of their break up. But the way his hand rested lightly
at the small of her back, its slow white curve and satin,
the way her eyes locked into his,
makes a liar of me.
Look, it's simple, they were in love.

And what I said before, that I wasn't surprised,
that's not true. Everything surprises me tonight,
mostly how much I've screwed up my life
with an almost infinite variety of lies.
They're all there. I'm able to see them,
turning faster and faster,
dancers who wobble
but hold on, hold on to each other.
And this is how I find myself,
unable tonight to stop envying
even a most temporary, simple tenderness,
and, without recourse,
having to love it from a distance
as it burns on hopeful and blind.

Cures

The part of the soul that doubts, again and again,
is scratchy as this song, "Mystery Train," where Elvis
relates some dark to himself. Even the light
in the living room seems sullen. We've turned the stereo
up loud, don't have to talk. After the latest argument,
trading blame is all that is left. After all that,
forgiveness? More punishment? Forgetting?
You curl, knees up, on the couch. Along your bare neck
the skin looks soft—shadows, the barrage
of falling brown hair, soft. I'm in the raggedy armchair,
and the music just washes through those questions,
then pours out the screen door. So this is what we do,
how we feel, each doubt a little larger
than desire, so that nothing
seems enough. And for a while,
ten minutes, I've stared at the album cover.
The face with the half-sneered, boyishly charming smile
stares back from the floor. The words echo wall to wall,
then silence as one song ends and we wait for the next.
What do we think? His smoothness and raveling wail will cure us
of all this? These rockabilly blues
from the early Memphis days, a shy country kid
opening for Pee Wee Crayton at the Flamingo Club.
When all he cared about was shouting the next tune.

The next tune. But endings are truer
for all their need: a mansion outside town,
years of Seconal, gaudy stage suits. Ways to simplify
the hundred confusions screaming in the body,
to become a star, or something stranger. . . .
I'd like to go over and brush away the hair
from your face. All the questions,

all the night, as it strikes
the house like a train whistle. And after I get up,
cross the room, you and I aren't sorry
it leads to this kiss. Or to what it brings on,
a soothing that lasts only so long,
like stardom
in America, or now this silence between songs.

The Temptations

Beyond, in a dusty lot,
two guys toss a baseball
back & forth,
a casually intense & loud
game of pepper. Each man
floats like a ball in dusk light.

I'm far enough inside myself
that I am not myself. Not a man
who notices most what's missing.
And, Jesus, whatever is not mine,
or gone, or stolen from me,
sticks in my throat,
so I'm forced to always talk about it.

Whoever complains as much as me
is in love with the sound of his own voice.
The sky presses a little on rooftops,
drops between homes,
rough stucco.
And whoever hears and believes me
is a fool for sickness
and unconvincing hope.

So now I just want to listen to music
climb
out my neighbor's windows. Soul records,
soul like a man shouting back
through the microphone of the dead,
as if it didn't matter much
at all, & it doesn't, that heaven
doesn't exist, no, it doesn't.

After

After the motorcycle lunged, past the intersection,
after the gymnast fell asleep on her tumble mat,
after the boy pulled his hand out, & no knife.
After the cop next door white-washed his adobe wall,
after the girl with birthday gifts rode a crowded escalator,
after the cats were found playing near a dune shack.
After the colander strained light from the kitchen window,
after the tractor looked less abandoned than the fog,
after the fog lifted off the broccoli flats.
After these, after each of these gave me good reason,
after every thing & every one else was safe.

There

Instead of the winter swallows, brown-gray
outside my bedroom window in the green
and gray salt cedar, now
in the long sweet nanosecond just before
I fall asleep,
I can hear the ragged breathing of someone I once held
rushing back from a muggy seacoast room. Along with
the rasp of waves demanding some ruthlessly nostalgic
insight into why we were together
for only that night. Memory,
gliding as it does
often enough to some regret.

Winter *should* be a long sentence—
the snow with great shyness
slowly raveling down.
Then it would be summer,
eventually, because snow melts
and we were dancing at the Town & Country Bar.
Some fast numbers, some slow.
A slim woman with long sandy hair.
What was odd
was that we'd been friends for years.
No, what was odd was the way we were both sure,
without saying a word,
that later we'd go to bed together.

We laughed about that
while we were undressing each other.
I had a sixty-mile drive to work
in the morning, and left before dawn.
I don't know if any of this matters as much
as the swallows outside.

I imagine it is the one winter night in Tucson
when it is cold enough, dark enough,
that I can't see who she or I
was back then. But we talk
for a while at the bar,
then the music goes from country-western
to Motown. We dance on the crowded floor
as if we're flying around on anything but legs,
and don't waste time, none at all,
getting there.

Walking By

They are all sleepy, & live around the block.
Soon to go in & bear one body each to bed.
For a few minutes more they talk. I listen.

I must be nine, leaning on a scabby birch that
Still seems protective. By the screened-in porch
A water sprinkler swings over cropped blue grass.

The mother bends & whispers to her husband,
The kids are ripping a baseball's seams,
And on the roof, tin angels, leftover

From Christmas, bunched & lost in thought.
Later, staring at the ceiling from my bed,
Then shutting my eyes, I see those angels,

Who might bolt at any time from their roost
And go out, hands in pockets, alone, walking,
And I think they will never stop, walking on

Through the coarse blue sky.

One Reason

If early one winter morning
you went to school after spending
the night with a greaser
and your wool sweater was
too light for the whipped breeze,
if you were sixteen that year
and never again, this bright day
early in 1971 you might clutch
History's brown books and Jane Eyre
in raw gloveless hands and feel
you had nothing to do with *them,*
that freaky girl lost in moors
or soldiers battling at Hastings.
You might, as she did, smoke
some Mexican pot with a guy
from homeroom, late in the day,
on the roof of his tenement house;
you might admire his new boots,
sharp black toes, ankle-high,
but keep stamping on them with
your glitzy platform heels,
dancing over the pebbled tar
and humming off-key.
                       She led
the boy through some damp sheets
reddened by sunset, lank on
the frayed clothesline, aerials
like steel bars of a cage dissolving.
Dared him a little closer
at the splintered ledge, and then
laughed when he wouldn't kiss.
She knew, as you would too,
this was the time to head home.

Where her father screamed and told
her, waving a steak knife,
if she ever got pregnant
he'd kill her, that simple.
It was simpler, what
she would do. Why shouldn't she,
name one reason? Just before Valentine's
Day, to ride a bus to the mall
and buy chocolates, eat them
that afternoon, the whole heart-
shaped red box gauded with
cupids on top, plump manic bodies
and glittery bows and arrows.
She gave her father his gift.
She hadn't put lipstick on—
he hated it—no makeup at all,
no mascara to make her eyes big,
as if something wondrous, or
terrifying, had leapt at her.
It was simple, he fumbled
with the wrapping, the lid,
and, there, huddled in tissue,
lay the dull, serrated blade.

The Wheel of the Hungry Is Turning

But no one in this bar hears,
Not one, & this bar, The
Buffet, flunks its name & feeds

No one, & none of us sees,
Though a young woman hikes up
Her blouse, lifts a child smaller

Than three months hypnotized
To her breast until baby
Sleeps again in her lap.

Smoking, eyeing the room, her
Husband straddles the next stool.
No one speaks to them, & she

Doesn't play Liar's Dice, can't
Shoot cutthroat, never mind pitch
Shuffleboard. This was her idea,

But right now she'd like to bolt.
Sure, sure, fine, says the husband—
Drunk, snarky—but why? can't you

Just relax? get loose, party
Some, you're all the time talking
You want to get out & meet

People, we don't see people.
Baby sleeps. Child of whatever
Impulses make these two stay, this

Middle-aged boy with beard
And dreadlocks, this woman pale
As her understandings, full

Of rocky good intentions.
These two stay. Now someone slams
Down a cup full of dice. Dice

Spill over the zinc counter,
Clattering, grungy, & over
Them swirl bar tunes, whispers, whoops,

Burps, sneezes, & avowals—
All the noises which drown out
The Wheel & keep it spinning,

Angry that it can't break us.

Secured Town

I don't have to tell this,
but, once, in a granite Quaker meeting house,
I listened to an ex-Army demo specialist with pulp for legs.
Cloaked in the ubiquitous fatigue jacket,
perched in his wheelchair, agitated,
agitating, unable to disarm his ties to a Vietnamese
woman dragged from a tin & corrugated cardboard barroom
into bush at the perimeter of a secured town.
This woman, who'd given the NVA
information, at least they suspected that,
pinned by two grunts for the squad leader.
So he could shove an illumination flare into her vagina.
Which was then ignited. I told you, right,
that fellow in his wheelchair had the habit of patting
his stomach with his calloused, nimble fingers?
Hinting a bag of acid-resistant plastic
replaced his intestines.
If I am still who I was before hearing that story,
if I am the person I was supposed to become,
then I'll say all of us in that hall wished to bathe
our faces with cool waters from the nearest font,
our hands impersonating the old ablutions,
imagining we deserve wholehearted mercy,
believing that forgetting suits us as we dreamily
walk in & out the doorways of bars & churches,
that instead of acid storms a mist will always arrive
outside our apartment walls, outside ballparks & newsstands
and kindergartens.
Though mercy lets us slip away,
I don't have to tell that,
not while I'm telling you this.

To the God

—after Cavafy

Eminence, blessed one—who always pretends
indifference to us, as if this were a long, slow
bus ride where you try to ignore the other
passengers, their chatter, all those souls burning
with the impeccably stylish grace of actors
on a twelve-inch black & white screen,
all burning to get to market—

                      well, are you pleased?
With this city, given us as punishment.
But weren't we to be abandoned, finally?
Actually, the life here is often marvelous.
We're all so driven, scrambling, for new toys,
enlightened kids, exotic menus, or some exquisite
and undiseased beauty slithering at our sides.
So our thanks, for giving us what we deserve.

The Judges in Us All

Whenever we stop talking on the phone tonight
I hear it. Not the humming, high-beam miles
of oily interstate between San Francisco and the Atlantic,
not fog horns or snowy wind
clattering through chopped corn stalks in Nebraska.
And if, at first, it *seems* to be the faint
buzz of gossipy teens
sharing a scrambled long-distance cable with us,
it is neither cute nor innocently malicious.
No, this sounds awful, crushing when it fills
the gaps in our talk. . . .

Just whispers really, but bullying,
inquisitorial, and not unlike the faceless, simpleminded
judges who have lately ruled hard
the lives of many of my friends. Is it your turn
tonight? is it *How did you become a fool*
whose heart drowns in its own dumb fluids?
Why so much pride? Why so desperate,
she loved you a shaky and punched-out love, pal,
and aren't you dead meat anyway? Who, who was she?

I don't know if you hear
them—I suspect you do. Brother,
I count on you, love your nerve,
because often hope is only nerve, the way
you toss off a remark
to sidestep the locomotive of their intent.
We hang up, walk outside,
under clouds badgering and abandoning the men
we have become.

The Fast Long Time

He'd always be glancing around.
The room in his eyes. Mostly it was crystal meth,
a brightness in the pupils, light
bouncing off a muddy river, almost righteous. Honey,
he'd say, I take good care of myself,
as if it were simply
an easy reply at a dull party.
I'm talking here about one in the Egyptian
wing of the museum, the white-arched hall
where he worked. Women & men standing
around cases of jewelry, a pharaoh's gardens
and zoo in clay dioramas. Laughter
rises above a jazz trio. A Christmas
party. They gossip, sip wine
from plastic cups, but he's a little bored
until the boy from shipping
comes on to him, imagining their clothes
thrown near the bed later,
the fast long time in bed,
so maybe he's not really listening. He's wearing
a mohair jacket, skinny gray leather tie,
and they're going to be ruined.
                                    Nothing
got to him. Not the men he went to bed with,
a faint groan on pale sheets.
What he'd hear was what he'd hear in his veins,
was a drum, long & fast, the heart, trailing off
to an empty parking lot
behind the loading dock. The shipper puts his arm
around Jimmy's waist, & shoves him to the gravel.
Two others jump out. Kicks to the head,
groin. Then they piss on him. Afterward they drop
him back of a rusting steel dumpster.

Now no answer.   Because, when his cheeks weren't
swollen & gauzed anymore, & after his jaw was unwired,
his face had the frozen, trapped look of someone
finished with the planet's rough trade.
Done, tagged, taken off display.
I don't know what he told himself then.
I know there are days almost all of us,
you, me, & all the other confused fools
believe we contrive our own fate & can take
what comes—then we get it,
like Jimmy did. Or we get away with whatever we want.
So maybe you're right,
maybe we're not being rushed toward a long silence
as if we were animals near a river—high whitish reeds,
things flushed by loud beaters
into the great iron cages of the king's zookeeper.
Then again maybe someone, something, is leaning now,
whispering, *Want to leave?*
Come on, let's get out of here.

Simon Says

At the end of a long dank trail cut by spring rains.
Steamy, bright, the first day
hot enough to lure out bunches of people.

In the park loud men, ringed in circles, bounce
scruffy cloth balls off their shoeless feet,
while a Doberman I watch,
sleek ugly carelessness, ears bandaged, a pup, romps
mindless of young couples who lounge and court on quilted rugs
and who wear little except street-smart shades,
though I am led to believe
that no heedlessness, no love or nakedness, not even
cold hate will hold back what happens
next. Because as the dog vanishes
the guy camped on a nearby blanket starts something.

Five years old, maybe four, a little girl
stands, demure, raggedy, glued to his side.
He pushes her toward me. His fingernails, bitten down,
painted black, chirp at her shoulders,
and now she gets the giggles.
                    O yes, won't any
impending mortal weirdness make us ready our armor?
Put yours on.
                    I put on a bored grin.
The little girl clamps two clenched fists
over her rosy ears, while father tells his baby to
go kiss some stranger. *Go ahead, he likes you,*
go french-kiss him, louder now,
like one kid bossing another, a game, Simon Says
go ahead, he ain't never been by someone pretty as you.
Then she looks at me and . . . nothing,
I wake sweating, cramped, on the couch
where I fell asleep reading. Just a bad dream.
And dawn's already come, light so summer-rich and fond
that a village hush spreads over crowded city roofs.

Except I find myself listening, for something.
Because suddenly I know.
I know I'd switched before I woke.
I'd whispered in her ear. I was her father,
and who was he but that drunk woman last night
South of Market, who offered to sell me her daughter.

Put off armor,
I wait for someone to tell me. It isn't possible
to forgive us all. Neither is it
impossible, but that is the other dream.

Zeus and Apollo

Written on clapboard or asbestos siding, the cartoony
spray-paint signatures of Apollo and Zeus,
two home boys out bombing last night in thick fog.
Fog near the shade of pearls. Except they didn't see the mist
that way, glad for their thin leather gloves.
Wind raw at the wide avenue, so they cut
from there to here.
                Even if this is in the past
tense, tense of the totally chilled-out,
even if they argued here over Krylon blue or candy-apple red,
that doesn't mean they knocked-off and streaked home then.
And if I saw fog the shade of pearls
it doesn't mean my heart in its own corrosive and healing fog
can't tug on thin leather gloves and stand
in front of a wall, pissing off the Fates
and whoever else owns that wall. Whoever owns it
means less than the dry, fallen leaves of eucalyptus
blown crackling over tar and concrete
and sounding, when you shut your eyes, like every tree
bursting into leaf for the first time, speeded-up
like the first minute of the world.

Masks

If tonight tells me to make my first & last choice,
Then I will rid myself of pride,

And anything else which would trick me so I forgot
My great, stammering need for spring,
For the patinas of cottonwood & palo verde bark,
For flash floods & the shrinking
Slab of rock stone my shadow carves.
I will get rid of it
Because, in this Tucson barrio, the Yaquis, city indians,
Go on with their jumbled, time-collapsing
Script of the Passion. Judas & the *Phariseos*
Steal baby Jesus & hustle from the manger.
Between the fry bread stands & Mission chapel,
In a mesquite ramada, the Deer Dancer,
Antlers tied to his brow,
Bandana of white silk
Which nearly covers his eyes, crooks his face to the roof,
Nostrils quivering, quizzing the air
As he chants & shuffles toward dawn,
When an old woman will grab back the Savior.

Then, kerosene fumes, matches, enveloping flames,
And, once again,
They'll toss Judas & friends on the bonfire.

What good is pride
When I have to choose, & choosing, take my mask,
My face,
From among cartoon characters
Or the demigods of last year's movies,
As these men do, these ogres, assistants to Judas, *chapayaquas*,
Boneyard clowns,
Who circle the ramada. It would be easier not to,
But I'd rather take their side.

55

The leader, wearing a Darth Vader helmet,
And his lieutenant, whose mask
Crosses Fred Flintstone's face with a cloud demon's,
Conniving, theatrical, taunting the Deer Dancer
As they guzzle his sweet-water & shake
Their hip rattles & fart, poking each other in glee,
Uncontaminated
Mirth, men whose names will be dispersed by smoke & ash,
Then gathered by the bougainvillea.

"Like an enormous yes"

—Philip Larkin

Even if there's no good day to die,
the day after should always be like this:
chill wind, fog begging each San Franciscan

to pretend that it's one of Hardy's scenic
rock-bottom times. While, downhill,
a gold-splotched German shepherd humps

a spindly bitch. So five bunched-up
blue and purple and red umbrellas tilt
just before ganging their bus, watching

this show. Let all the slick colors mix
then to void-sweet black. So what.
Because there's jazz, or blues to finesse

the passage, glint off a trumpet cone
calling briefly, calling love. Brief love
along streets that betray. Always

that fire, even when you can't see it.

Leaving the Gateway Cinema

While my wife & I watched the movie it rained outside.
The air glistens, washed, & now it's colder.
Our first breaths steam. Across from the chrome theater lobby
and the lush, annihilating parable of Martin Guerre, put on trial
day after medieval French day for claiming he's someone
he isn't, pain now worth five dollars each,
across the cobblestones, there's an expensive café.
Warm faces lean over candles & fluted wine glasses,
marble tables on a black & white tiled floor.
Café Ciao. Sometimes, like tonight, it looks to me
like a gameboard in a dream, that floor.
Those people, their mouths going *Your move,*
No, yours.

Then, Lord, one of your Vietnamese, a woman,
runs up to me. Blue shrunken sweatshirt & cords,
deeply wrinkled at the eyes, what I claim must have
once been a beautiful, enviable face now a mask.
Hundreds like her in the city. In Tenderloin crone
hotels, & the kids, begging, shrill, annoyed, take out your heart.
Like them, she wants to sell us back ours
as garlic, plastic baggies of garlic
the size of a ten-year-old's fist.
Look, we'll take some—though I'm tempted to tell her
I'm sick of taking, of wanting, & that includes all stuff
from the garden. What about the city's faith in pleasure,
the commandment *Crave more so you stay happy,*
as if the glow from sunlight, from neon
and streetlights, could pull us
right out of ourselves, when I see us caught

now, held in nothing, in the fashionable department
store windows. Along with the life-sized, strutting
dolls posed there. Michaela reaching
for my hand, me tossing a bag of garlic.

58

When that woman handed over our bag
and grabbed a buck from my fingers, I swear, she was someone
trying to snatch something back. Her old life,
somebody she loved, maybe just a moment
when the fighting stopped & the countryside & rivers
in huge anticipation of pleasure came home.
But that's movieland bullshit too.
When I think of all we have to lose,
all that pleasure asks us to settle for,
and I can't recall I ever wanted so much, I know
I'm hiding something.
Lord, tell me, who are we? What's really ours?

For Michaela

After this graveyard shift, the escape I want
is not on these mostly deserted streets
that fog makes blank as a rain-warped drive-in screen.
So instead I listen to cabbie Frank daMotta as he
drives me home. His story tonight about three blacks
from Hunter's Point who hijacked & robbed him
after pickup, crosstown at a rumpled wedding reception,
each wearing a crushed velvet, baby blue tux.
His head nods, & his teenage daughter's face nods
inside the little schoolroom photo stapled on back
of his Giants baseball cap, until she fills
all four corners of the screen before me.
She too asks for release & asks & asks everyone.
And I mumble *un-huh, un-huh,* thinking only of walking
in the dark down the length of our house
to where you're asleep with your own hunger.
All spring there's been only that sweet thought,
and now, we love so irretrievably that it's
like the cab rolling in third down the hill,
and Frank daMotta's daughter with her round blue eyes
and solemn wide mouth staring back, pleading, don't
murder my father or rob his earnings, don't take
anything. Just go home. Go home!

Arrival Song

Here I am — on the eve of overtaking my thirty-third year,
up alone, pacing, my father's favorite act of contrition,
though he seldom confesses, & never any sins, & why should he?
since he once lingered walking over the Brightman Street Bridge
and spit into water on fire with a dusk light so valedictory
that the obstinate blood in his veins decreed
he should chain himself, for the rest of his days,
to that city, mill-owned & parish-divided, by the flaming river,
where I'd be born, where, after he'd met my mother,
after they'd danced to big bands at amusement park ballrooms,
after he'd sat up in bed in the dark smoking Pall Malls
trying to call up her skin, lemon soap, swaying legs, then,
my father began inventing a son, an outline four inches
taller than he, over-educated, with the same smart mouth
and vanities, who, some future late fall night, would stop
pacing the studio he sublets from a summer painter,
in a beach town tricked out with strings of Christmas bulbs,
crèche scenes, all tinsel & plywood goats & camels,
stopping now & staring at one canvas, the terrible conclusion
to how many hours of unsurprised, empty-headed attempts
at abstract expressionism, pure blankness until on closer look
I notice groups of black & white photos were cut-out
and collaged beneath the splashed brush strokes,
under the violet & crimson & pink acrylics, men stroking cocks
or entering women from behind, leering like donkeys,
two teenage Japanese girls fingering each other,
choked glimpses of scrotum, breasts, a half-dozen
groping & braying in what the artist titles "Heaven,"
all of them splashed by blotched shades of pink paint,
of crimson & violet, so that when I step back a few feet
they dissolve, & go on dissolving, into colors I'll walk
through tomorrow, twilight, hiking with Victoria
in a brambled stretch of Truro, back of ocean cliffs, when we
suddenly catch a glimpse of an osprey, blue clawed, white hooded,
riding thermals in loosening steady circles above the water,
wheeling, sure, arresting, awed, with no illusions.

About the Author

David Rivard was born in Fall River, Massachusetts, in 1953.
He was educated at Southeastern Massachusetts University and
Princeton University, where he studied anthropology, and at the
University of Arizona, where he received an M.F.A. in Creative
Writing. In 1986 he was the recipient of a poetry fellowship from
the National Endowment for the Arts, and he has twice been a
writing fellow at the Fine Arts Work Center in Provincetown. A
lecturer in English at Tufts University, he lives in Arlington,
Massachusetts.

PITT POETRY SERIES
Ed Ochester, General Editor

Dannie Abse, *Collected Poems*
Claribel Alegría, *Flowers from the Volcano*
Claribel Alegría, *Woman of the River*
Maggie Anderson, *Cold Comfort*
Michael Benedikt, *The Badminton at Great Barrington; Or, Gustave Mahler & the Chattanooga Choo-Choo*
Michael Burkard, *Ruby for Grief*
Siv Cedering, *Letters from the Floating World*
Lorna Dee Cervantes, *Emplumada*
Robert Coles, *A Festering Sweetness: Poems of American People*
Kate Daniels, *The Niobe Poems*
Kate Daniels, *The White Wave*
Norman Dubie, *Alehouse Sonnets*
Stuart Dybek, *Brass Knuckles*
Odysseus Elytis, *The Axion Esti*
Jane Flanders, *Timepiece*
Gary Gildner, *Blue Like the Heavens: New & Selected Poems*
Bruce Guernsey, *January Thaw*
Michael S. Harper, *Song: I Want a Witness*
Barbara Helfgott Hyett, *In Evidence: Poems of the Liberation of Nazi Concentration Camps*
Milne Holton and Paul Vangelisti, eds., *The New Polish Poetry: A Bilingual Collection*
David Huddle, *Paper Boy*
Phyllis Janowitz, *Temporary Dwellings*
Lawrence Joseph, *Curriculum Vitae*
Lawrence Joseph, *Shouting at No One*
Etheridge Knight, *The Essential Etheridge Knight*
Ted Kooser, *One World at a Time*
Ted Kooser, *Sure Signs: New and Selected Poems*
Larry Levis, *Winter Stars*
Larry Levis, *Wrecking Crew*
Robert Louthan, *Living in Code*
Tom Lowenstein, tr., *Eskimo Poems from Canada and Greenland*